50 Vegetarian Recipes for Home

By: Kelly Johnson

Table of Contents

- Lentil Soup
- Chickpea Curry
- Stuffed Bell Peppers
- Veggie Stir-Fry
- Black Bean Tacos
- Spinach Quiche
- Cauliflower Rice
- Sweet Potato Chili
- Mushroom Risotto
- Eggplant Parmesan
- Greek Salad
- Butternut Squash Soup
- Veggie Burgers
- Zucchini Noodles
- Chickpea Salad
- Vegetable Frittata
- Tofu Stir-Fry
- Carrot and Hummus Wrap
- Roasted Veggie Bowl
- Quinoa Salad
- Tomato Basil Soup
- Avocado Toast
- Kale and White Bean Stew
- Stuffed Acorn Squash
- Veggie Sushi Rolls
- Sweet Potato Fries
- Creamy Tomato Pasta
- Vegetable Curry
- Beet Salad
- Portobello Mushroom Tacos
- Corn and Black Bean Salad
- Vegan Burritos

- Green Smoothie Bowl
- Ratatouille
- Spaghetti Squash Primavera
- Lentil Loaf
- Roasted Brussels Sprouts
- Veggie Wraps
- Thai Peanut Noodles
- Falafel
- Sweet Potato and Black Bean Enchiladas
- Cauliflower Steaks
- Green Bean Almondine
- Vegan Shepherd's Pie
- Mediterranean Quinoa Bowl
- Broccoli Cheddar Soup
- Spinach and Feta Stuffed Mushrooms
- Lentil and Vegetable Stew
- Tomato and Mozzarella Panini
- Apple and Walnut Salad

Lentil Soup

Ingredients:

- 1 tablespoon olive oil
- 1 onion, diced
- 2 carrots, diced
- 2 celery stalks, diced
- 3 cloves garlic, minced
- 1 1/2 cups dried lentils, rinsed
- 1 can (14.5 oz) diced tomatoes
- 6 cups vegetable or chicken broth
- 1 bay leaf
- 1 teaspoon dried thyme
- Salt and pepper to taste
- 2 cups chopped spinach or kale (optional)

Instructions:

1. Heat olive oil in a large pot over medium heat. Add onion, carrots, and celery, and cook until softened, about 5 minutes.
2. Stir in garlic and cook for another minute.
3. Add lentils, diced tomatoes, broth, bay leaf, and thyme. Bring to a boil.
4. Reduce heat and simmer, uncovered, for 25-30 minutes or until lentils are tender.
5. Season with salt and pepper to taste. If using spinach or kale, stir it in during the last 5 minutes of cooking.
6. Remove bay leaf before serving. Enjoy hot.

Chickpea Curry

Ingredients:

- 2 tablespoons olive oil
- 1 onion, finely chopped
- 3 cloves garlic, minced
- 1 tablespoon ginger, minced
- 2 tablespoons curry powder
- 1 teaspoon ground cumin
- 1/2 teaspoon turmeric
- 1 can (14.5 oz) diced tomatoes
- 1 can (15 oz) chickpeas, drained and rinsed
- 1 can (14 oz) coconut milk
- 1 cup spinach or kale (optional)
- Salt and pepper to taste
- Fresh cilantro for garnish

Instructions:

1. Heat olive oil in a large pan over medium heat. Add onion and cook until soft, about 5 minutes.
2. Stir in garlic and ginger, and cook for 1 minute.
3. Add curry powder, cumin, and turmeric, and cook for 1-2 minutes until fragrant.
4. Add diced tomatoes and cook for 5 minutes, allowing flavors to meld.
5. Stir in chickpeas and coconut milk, and bring to a simmer. Cook for 10-15 minutes, until thickened.
6. Add spinach or kale, if using, and cook until wilted.
7. Season with salt and pepper to taste. Garnish with fresh cilantro before serving.

Stuffed Bell Peppers

Ingredients:

- 4 bell peppers (any color)
- 1 lb ground beef or turkey
- 1 cup cooked rice
- 1 can (14.5 oz) diced tomatoes
- 1 small onion, chopped
- 2 cloves garlic, minced
- 1 cup shredded cheese (cheddar or mozzarella)
- 1 tsp dried oregano
- 1 tsp dried basil
- Salt and pepper to taste

Instructions:

1. Preheat oven to 375°F (190°C).
2. Cut the tops off the bell peppers and remove seeds and membranes.
3. In a skillet, cook ground meat with onion and garlic until browned. Drain fat.
4. Stir in cooked rice, diced tomatoes, oregano, basil, salt, and pepper. Cook for 5 minutes.
5. Stuff the peppers with the mixture and place them upright in a baking dish.
6. Top with shredded cheese.
7. Bake for 30-35 minutes, until peppers are tender and cheese is melted.

Enjoy!

Veggie Stir-Fry

Ingredients:

- 2 tbsp vegetable oil (or any oil with a high smoke point)
- 1 onion, sliced
- 2-3 cloves garlic, minced
- 1 bell pepper, sliced
- 1 cup broccoli florets
- 1 cup snap peas or green beans
- 1 carrot, sliced thinly
- 1 cup mushrooms, sliced (optional)
- 1/4 cup soy sauce or tamari
- 2 tbsp hoisin sauce (optional)
- 1 tbsp rice vinegar or lemon juice
- 1 tsp grated ginger (optional)
- 1 tbsp cornstarch mixed with 2 tbsp water (for thickening, optional)
- Cooked rice or noodles for serving
- Sesame seeds and sliced green onions for garnish (optional)

Instructions:

1. **Prep Ingredients:** Wash and cut all vegetables. Mix the cornstarch and water if using.
2. **Heat Oil:** In a large pan or wok, heat vegetable oil over medium-high heat.
3. **Cook Aromatics:** Add sliced onion and cook for 2-3 minutes until translucent. Add minced garlic (and grated ginger if using) and cook for another 30 seconds until fragrant.
4. **Stir-Fry Vegetables:** Add bell pepper, broccoli, snap peas, and carrot to the pan. Stir-fry for about 5-7 minutes, or until vegetables are tender-crisp.
5. **Add Sauce:** Pour in soy sauce, hoisin sauce (if using), and rice vinegar. Stir to combine and cook for another 1-2 minutes.
6. **Thicken Sauce:** If you want a thicker sauce, add the cornstarch mixture to the pan and stir until the sauce thickens.
7. **Serve:** Serve the stir-fry over cooked rice or noodles. Garnish with sesame seeds and sliced green onions if desired.

Feel free to adjust the vegetables based on what you have on hand or your personal preferences. Enjoy your stir-fry!

Black Bean Tacos

Ingredients:

For the Tacos:

- 1 can (15 oz) black beans, drained and rinsed
- 1 tbsp olive oil
- 1 small onion, diced
- 2 cloves garlic, minced
- 1 bell pepper, diced
- 1 tsp ground cumin
- 1 tsp chili powder
- 1/2 tsp paprika
- 1/2 tsp smoked paprika (optional)
- Salt and pepper to taste
- 8 small taco tortillas or 4 larger ones

For Toppings (optional but recommended):

- 1 cup shredded lettuce
- 1 cup diced tomatoes
- 1 avocado, sliced or mashed
- 1/2 cup shredded cheese (cheddar, Monterey Jack, or your choice)
- 1/4 cup chopped fresh cilantro
- Lime wedges
- Salsa or hot sauce

Instructions:

1. **Prepare the Filling:**
    - Heat olive oil in a large skillet over medium heat.
    - Add diced onion and cook until translucent, about 3-4 minutes.
    - Stir in minced garlic and cook for another 30 seconds.
    - Add diced bell pepper and cook for 3-4 minutes until softened.
    - Stir in black beans, cumin, chili powder, paprika, smoked paprika (if using), salt, and pepper.
    - Cook for another 5-7 minutes, stirring occasionally, until the beans are heated through and the flavors have melded together.
2. **Warm the Tortillas:**
    - Heat the taco tortillas according to package instructions, or warm them in a dry skillet over medium heat for about 30 seconds on each side, until pliable.
3. **Assemble the Tacos:**
    - Spoon the black bean mixture onto the tortillas.

- Top with your choice of shredded lettuce, diced tomatoes, avocado, cheese, and chopped cilantro.
4. **Serve:**
    - Serve with lime wedges and salsa or hot sauce on the side.

Enjoy your tasty and nutritious black bean tacos!

Spinach Quiche

Ingredients:

For the Crust:

- 1 1/2 cups all-purpose flour
- 1/2 cup unsalted butter, cold and cut into pieces
- 1/4 tsp salt
- 2-3 tbsp cold water

For the Filling:

- 2 cups fresh spinach, chopped
- 1/2 cup diced onion
- 1 cup shredded cheese (cheddar, Swiss, or your choice)
- 4 large eggs
- 1 cup half-and-half or milk
- 1/4 tsp nutmeg (optional)
- Salt and pepper to taste

Instructions:

1. **Prepare the Crust:**
   - Preheat oven to 375°F (190°C).
   - In a food processor, combine flour, butter, and salt until the mixture resembles coarse crumbs.
   - Gradually add cold water, one tablespoon at a time, until the dough comes together.
   - Press the dough into a 9-inch pie pan. Prick the bottom with a fork.
   - Bake for 10 minutes, then remove from oven and set aside.
2. **Prepare the Filling:**
   - Sauté onions in a skillet over medium heat until translucent. Add spinach and cook until wilted. Set aside.
   - In a bowl, whisk together eggs, half-and-half, nutmeg (if using), salt, and pepper.
   - Stir in the cheese and spinach mixture.
3. **Assemble and Bake:**
   - Pour the filling into the pre-baked crust.
   - Bake for 30-35 minutes, or until the quiche is set and lightly golden on top.
4. **Cool and Serve:**
   - Let the quiche cool for a few minutes before slicing. Enjoy warm or at room temperature!

Feel free to add other ingredients like mushrooms or bacon for extra flavor!

Cauliflower Rice

Ingredients:

- 1 head of cauliflower
- 1-2 tbsp olive oil
- Salt and pepper to taste
- Optional: garlic powder, onion powder, or herbs for extra flavor

Instructions:

1. **Prepare the Cauliflower:**
   - Remove the leaves and stem from the cauliflower and cut it into florets.
2. **Rice the Cauliflower:**
   - Use a food processor to pulse the cauliflower florets until they resemble rice grains. Alternatively, you can grate the cauliflower using a box grater.
3. **Cook the Cauliflower Rice:**
   - Heat olive oil in a large skillet over medium heat.
   - Add the riced cauliflower and cook for 5-7 minutes, stirring occasionally, until tender and slightly golden.
   - Season with salt, pepper, and any optional seasonings.
4. **Serve:**
   - Serve as you would regular rice, with your favorite dishes.

Enjoy this versatile and healthy side!

Sweet Potato Chili

Ingredients:

- 1 tbsp olive oil
- 1 onion, diced
- 2 cloves garlic, minced
- 1 bell pepper, diced
- 2 medium sweet potatoes, peeled and diced
- 1 can (15 oz) diced tomatoes
- 1 can (15 oz) black beans, drained and rinsed
- 1 can (15 oz) kidney beans, drained and rinsed
- 2 cups vegetable or chicken broth
- 2 tbsp chili powder
- 1 tsp cumin
- 1/2 tsp smoked paprika (optional)
- Salt and pepper to taste

Instructions:

1. **Sauté Vegetables:**
    - Heat olive oil in a large pot over medium heat.
    - Add onion and cook until translucent, about 3-4 minutes.
    - Stir in garlic and cook for another 30 seconds.
2. **Cook Sweet Potatoes:**
    - Add bell pepper and sweet potatoes. Cook for 5 minutes, stirring occasionally.
3. **Add Remaining Ingredients:**
    - Stir in diced tomatoes, black beans, kidney beans, broth, chili powder, cumin, smoked paprika (if using), salt, and pepper.
4. **Simmer:**
    - Bring to a boil, then reduce heat and simmer for 25-30 minutes, or until sweet potatoes are tender.
5. **Serve:**
    - Serve hot, garnished with your favorite toppings like cilantro, avocado, or cheese.

Enjoy your comforting and nutritious chili!

Mushroom Risotto

Ingredients:

- 1 tbsp olive oil
- 1 small onion, finely chopped
- 2 cloves garlic, minced
- 1 cup arborio rice
- 1 cup white wine (optional)
- 4 cups chicken or vegetable broth, kept warm
- 2 cups mushrooms, sliced (cremini, shiitake, or button)
- 1/2 cup grated Parmesan cheese
- 2 tbsp butter
- Salt and pepper to taste
- Fresh parsley, chopped (optional)

Instructions:

1. **Sauté Mushrooms:**
   - Heat olive oil in a large pan over medium heat. Add mushrooms and cook until browned and tender. Set aside.
2. **Cook Aromatics:**
   - In the same pan, add a bit more oil if needed. Sauté onion until translucent, about 3-4 minutes. Stir in garlic and cook for another 30 seconds.
3. **Add Rice:**
   - Add arborio rice and cook, stirring frequently, for 2 minutes until the rice is slightly translucent around the edges.
4. **Deglaze with Wine:**
   - Pour in white wine, if using, and cook until it's mostly absorbed.
5. **Add Broth:**
   - Begin adding warm broth one ladleful at a time, stirring constantly. Wait until the liquid is mostly absorbed before adding more. Continue until rice is creamy and cooked to your liking, about 18-20 minutes.
6. **Finish Risotto:**
   - Stir in sautéed mushrooms, Parmesan cheese, and butter. Season with salt and pepper to taste.
7. **Serve:**
   - Garnish with fresh parsley if desired and serve hot.

Enjoy this creamy, savory dish!

Eggplant Parmesan

Ingredients:

- 2 medium eggplants, sliced into 1/4-inch rounds
- Salt
- 1 cup all-purpose flour
- 2 large eggs, beaten
- 2 cups breadcrumbs (Italian or plain)
- 2 cups marinara sauce
- 1 1/2 cups shredded mozzarella cheese
- 1/2 cup grated Parmesan cheese
- 2 tbsp olive oil
- Fresh basil or parsley for garnish (optional)

Instructions:

1. **Prepare Eggplant:**
   - Preheat oven to 375°F (190°C). Sprinkle eggplant slices with salt and let sit for 30 minutes to draw out moisture. Rinse and pat dry with paper towels.
2. **Bread the Eggplant:**
   - Dredge each eggplant slice in flour, dip in beaten eggs, then coat with breadcrumbs.
3. **Cook the Eggplant:**
   - Heat olive oil in a large skillet over medium heat. Fry eggplant slices until golden brown, about 2-3 minutes per side. Drain on paper towels.
4. **Assemble:**
   - Spread a thin layer of marinara sauce in a baking dish. Arrange a layer of eggplant slices on top, then spread some marinara sauce over them. Sprinkle with mozzarella and Parmesan cheese. Repeat layers until ingredients are used up, ending with cheese.
5. **Bake:**
   - Bake for 25-30 minutes, or until the cheese is melted and bubbly and the eggplant is tender.
6. **Garnish and Serve:**
   - Let cool slightly before garnishing with fresh basil or parsley. Serve hot.

Enjoy your delicious eggplant Parmesan!

Greek Salad

Ingredients:

- 3 cups cherry tomatoes, halved (or 2 large tomatoes, chopped)
- 1 cucumber, peeled and sliced
- 1/2 red onion, thinly sliced
- 1/2 cup Kalamata olives, pitted
- 1/2 cup feta cheese, crumbled
- 1/4 cup extra-virgin olive oil
- 2 tbsp red wine vinegar
- 1 tsp dried oregano
- Salt and pepper to taste
- Fresh parsley or basil for garnish (optional)

Instructions:

1. **Prepare the Vegetables:**
   - In a large salad bowl, combine cherry tomatoes, cucumber, red onion, and Kalamata olives.
2. **Add Cheese:**
   - Top with crumbled feta cheese.
3. **Make the Dressing:**
   - In a small bowl, whisk together olive oil, red wine vinegar, dried oregano, salt, and pepper.
4. **Toss the Salad:**
   - Pour the dressing over the salad and toss gently to coat all the ingredients.
5. **Garnish and Serve:**
   - Garnish with fresh parsley or basil if desired. Serve immediately or chill in the refrigerator for 30 minutes to let the flavors meld.

This Greek salad is perfect on its own or as a side dish with grilled meats or pita bread. Enjoy!

Butternut Squash Soup

Ingredients:

- 1 large butternut squash (about 2 lbs), peeled, seeded, and cubed
- 2 tbsp olive oil
- 1 onion, chopped
- 2 cloves garlic, minced
- 1 carrot, chopped
- 1 celery stalk, chopped
- 4 cups vegetable or chicken broth
- 1/2 cup coconut milk or heavy cream
- 1 tsp ground cumin
- 1/2 tsp ground nutmeg
- Salt and pepper to taste
- Optional: 1 apple, peeled and chopped (for a hint of sweetness)
- Fresh thyme or parsley for garnish (optional)

Instructions:

1. **Roast the Squash:**
    - Preheat your oven to 400°F (200°C). Toss the cubed butternut squash with 1 tablespoon of olive oil and season with salt and pepper. Spread in a single layer on a baking sheet.
    - Roast for 25-30 minutes, or until the squash is tender and lightly browned. Set aside.
2. **Cook the Vegetables:**
    - In a large pot, heat the remaining 1 tablespoon of olive oil over medium heat.
    - Add the onion, garlic, carrot, and celery. Cook for 5-7 minutes, or until the vegetables are softened and the onion is translucent.
3. **Combine and Simmer:**
    - Add the roasted butternut squash to the pot. Stir in the vegetable or chicken broth and bring to a boil.
    - Reduce heat and let simmer for 10-15 minutes to allow the flavors to meld.
4. **Blend the Soup:**
    - Use an immersion blender to puree the soup until smooth. Alternatively, carefully transfer the soup in batches to a countertop blender.
5. **Finish the Soup:**
    - Stir in the coconut milk or heavy cream, ground cumin, nutmeg, and adjust seasoning with salt and pepper.
6. **Serve:**
    - Garnish with fresh thyme or parsley if desired. Serve hot.

Enjoy this creamy and satisfying soup!

Veggie Burgers

Ingredients:

- 1 can (15 oz) black beans, drained and rinsed
- 1 cup cooked quinoa (or cooked rice)
- 1/2 cup finely chopped onion
- 1/2 cup finely chopped bell pepper
- 2 cloves garlic, minced
- 1/2 cup breadcrumbs (or oats for a gluten-free option)
- 1 egg (or flax egg for vegan option: 1 tbsp flaxseed meal + 2.5 tbsp water, mixed and let sit for 5 minutes)
- 1 tsp ground cumin
- 1 tsp smoked paprika
- 1/2 tsp chili powder
- Salt and pepper to taste
- 2 tbsp olive oil (for cooking)

Instructions:

1. **Prepare the Mixture:**
   - In a large bowl, mash the black beans with a fork or potato masher, leaving some chunks for texture.
   - Stir in the cooked quinoa (or rice), onion, bell pepper, garlic, breadcrumbs, egg, cumin, smoked paprika, chili powder, salt, and pepper. Mix until well combined.
2. **Form Patties:**
   - Divide the mixture into 4-6 portions and shape into patties, pressing firmly to hold together.
3. **Cook the Patties:**
   - Heat olive oil in a large skillet over medium heat.
   - Cook the patties for 5-6 minutes on each side, or until they are golden brown and crispy on the outside.
4. **Serve:**
   - Serve the veggie burgers on buns with your favorite toppings and condiments, such as lettuce, tomato, avocado, pickles, and your favorite sauce or mustard.

Optional Add-Ins:

- **Cheese:** Top with a slice of cheese (cheddar, Swiss, or vegan cheese) during the last minute of cooking.
- **Spices and Herbs:** Add fresh herbs like cilantro or parsley, or spices like curry powder or garlic powder for additional flavor.

Enjoy your delicious and customizable veggie burgers!

Zucchini Noodles

Ingredients:

- 2-3 medium zucchinis
- 1-2 tbsp olive oil
- Salt and pepper to taste
- Optional: minced garlic, crushed red pepper flakes, or herbs like basil or parsley

Instructions:

1. **Prepare the Zucchini:**
   - Wash the zucchinis and cut off the ends.
   - Use a spiralizer to create noodles. If you don't have a spiralizer, you can use a julienne peeler or a regular vegetable peeler to make thin strips.
2. **Cook the Noodles:**
   - Heat olive oil in a large skillet over medium heat.
   - Add the zucchini noodles and cook, stirring occasionally, for 3-5 minutes until they are tender but still slightly crisp. Be careful not to overcook, as they can become mushy.
3. **Season:**
   - Season with salt and pepper to taste. If you like, add minced garlic or red pepper flakes for extra flavor. Cook for an additional 1-2 minutes if adding garlic.
4. **Serve:**
   - Serve the zucchini noodles with your favorite sauce, such as marinara, pesto, or a light lemon vinaigrette.

Tips:

- **Drain Excess Moisture:** If you're not serving immediately, you might want to pat the noodles dry with paper towels to remove excess moisture that can accumulate during cooking.
- **Pre-Salting:** For even firmer noodles, you can toss the spiralized zucchini with a little salt and let it sit for 10-15 minutes before cooking. This helps draw out some moisture.

Enjoy your healthy and versatile zucchini noodles!

Chickpea Salad

Ingredients:

- 1 can (15 oz) chickpeas, drained and rinsed (or about 1 1/2 cups cooked chickpeas)
- 1 cucumber, diced
- 1 bell pepper, diced
- 1/2 red onion, finely chopped
- 1 cup cherry tomatoes, halved
- 1/4 cup fresh parsley, chopped (or cilantro if you prefer)
- 1/4 cup crumbled feta cheese (optional)
- 1/4 cup olives, pitted and sliced (optional)

For the Dressing:

- 3 tbsp extra-virgin olive oil
- 2 tbsp red wine vinegar or lemon juice
- 1 tsp Dijon mustard
- 1 clove garlic, minced
- 1/2 tsp dried oregano
- Salt and pepper to taste

Instructions:

1. **Prepare the Vegetables:**
   - In a large bowl, combine the chickpeas, cucumber, bell pepper, red onion, cherry tomatoes, and parsley.
2. **Prepare the Dressing:**
   - In a small bowl or jar, whisk together the olive oil, red wine vinegar (or lemon juice), Dijon mustard, minced garlic, dried oregano, salt, and pepper until well combined.
3. **Combine:**
   - Pour the dressing over the salad and toss gently to coat all the ingredients evenly.
4. **Add Optional Ingredients:**
   - If using, sprinkle crumbled feta cheese and olives over the top and give the salad a final gentle toss.
5. **Serve:**
   - Serve immediately or chill in the refrigerator for 30 minutes to let the flavors meld.

Tips:

- **Customization:** Feel free to add other ingredients such as avocado, artichoke hearts, or chopped celery based on your preference.
- **Make Ahead:** This salad can be made ahead of time and stored in the refrigerator for up to 3 days. The flavors will continue to develop as it sits.

Enjoy your fresh and flavorful chickpea salad!

Vegetable Frittata

Ingredients:

- 1 tbsp olive oil
- 1 small onion, chopped
- 1 bell pepper, diced
- 1 cup spinach or kale, chopped
- 1 cup cherry tomatoes, halved (or diced regular tomatoes)
- 6 large eggs
- 1/2 cup milk or cream
- 1/2 cup shredded cheese (cheddar, feta, or your choice)
- Salt and pepper to taste
- 1 tsp dried oregano or basil (optional)

Instructions:

1. **Preheat Oven:**
   - Preheat your oven to 375°F (190°C).
2. **Cook the Vegetables:**
   - Heat olive oil in an ovenproof skillet over medium heat.
   - Add onion and cook until softened, about 3-4 minutes.
   - Add bell pepper and cook for another 3 minutes.
   - Stir in spinach or kale and cook until wilted. Add tomatoes and cook for 1-2 minutes.
3. **Prepare the Egg Mixture:**
   - In a bowl, whisk together eggs, milk, cheese, salt, pepper, and optional herbs.
4. **Combine and Cook:**
   - Pour the egg mixture over the vegetables in the skillet. Stir gently to combine.
5. **Bake:**
   - Transfer the skillet to the preheated oven and bake for 20-25 minutes, or until the frittata is set and lightly golden on top.
6. **Cool and Serve:**
   - Let the frittata cool for a few minutes before slicing. Serve warm or at room temperature.

Tips:

- **Customization:** Feel free to add other ingredients like mushrooms, zucchini, or cooked bacon or sausage.
- **Non-Stick Skillet:** Ensure your skillet is well-seasoned or use a non-stick pan to prevent sticking.

Enjoy your delicious and nutritious vegetable frittata!

Tofu Stir-Fry

Ingredients:

- 1 block firm or extra-firm tofu, drained and cubed
- 2 tbsp vegetable oil
- 1 bell pepper, sliced
- 1 cup broccoli florets
- 1 cup snap peas or green beans
- 1 carrot, sliced
- 2 cloves garlic, minced
- 1 tbsp ginger, minced (optional)
- 1/4 cup soy sauce or tamari
- 2 tbsp hoisin sauce (optional)
- 1 tbsp cornstarch mixed with 2 tbsp water (for thickening, optional)
- Cooked rice or noodles for serving
- Sesame seeds and sliced green onions for garnish (optional)

Instructions:

1. **Prepare the Tofu:**
   - Heat 1 tablespoon of vegetable oil in a large pan over medium-high heat. Add tofu cubes and cook until golden and crispy on all sides, about 7-10 minutes. Remove tofu and set aside.
2. **Stir-Fry Vegetables:**
   - In the same pan, add the remaining tablespoon of oil. Sauté garlic (and ginger if using) for 30 seconds until fragrant.
   - Add bell pepper, broccoli, snap peas, and carrot. Stir-fry for 5-7 minutes until vegetables are tender-crisp.
3. **Combine and Sauce:**
   - Return the tofu to the pan. Stir in soy sauce, hoisin sauce (if using), and cornstarch mixture (if using). Cook for another 1-2 minutes until the sauce thickens and everything is well-coated.
4. **Serve:**
   - Serve over cooked rice or noodles. Garnish with sesame seeds and sliced green onions if desired.

Enjoy your flavorful and satisfying tofu stir-fry!

Carrot and Hummus Wrap

Ingredients:

- 4 large whole wheat or spinach tortillas
- 1 cup hummus (store-bought or homemade)
- 2 large carrots, peeled and julienned or grated
- 1 cucumber, sliced thinly
- 1/2 red bell pepper, thinly sliced
- 1 cup spinach or mixed greens
- 1 avocado, sliced (optional)
- 1/4 cup red onion, thinly sliced (optional)
- Salt and pepper to taste
- Fresh lemon juice (optional)

Instructions:

1. **Prepare the Ingredients:**
   - Peel and julienne or grate the carrots.
   - Slice the cucumber, bell pepper, and avocado if using.
   - Wash and dry the spinach or mixed greens.
2. **Assemble the Wraps:**
   - Lay out the tortillas on a flat surface.
   - Spread a generous layer of hummus over each tortilla, leaving a small border around the edges.
   - Arrange the carrots, cucumber, bell pepper, spinach, and any additional vegetables evenly over the hummus.
   - Add avocado slices and red onion if using.
3. **Season:**
   - Sprinkle with salt, pepper, and a squeeze of lemon juice if desired.
4. **Roll the Wraps:**
   - Carefully fold in the sides of the tortilla, then roll it up tightly from the bottom.
5. **Serve:**
   - Cut the wraps in half diagonally and serve immediately, or wrap them in foil or parchment paper for a portable lunch.

Tips:

- **Add Protein:** For extra protein, add some cooked chickpeas, grilled chicken, or feta cheese.
- **Spice it Up:** Add a dash of hot sauce or a sprinkle of your favorite herbs for added flavor.

Enjoy your nutritious and delicious carrot and hummus wraps!

Roasted Veggie Bowl

Ingredients:

- 4 large whole wheat or spinach tortillas
- 1 cup hummus (store-bought or homemade)
- 2 large carrots, peeled and julienned or grated
- 1 cucumber, sliced thinly
- 1/2 red bell pepper, thinly sliced
- 1 cup spinach or mixed greens
- 1 avocado, sliced (optional)
- 1/4 cup red onion, thinly sliced (optional)
- Salt and pepper to taste
- Fresh lemon juice (optional)

Instructions:

1. **Prepare the Ingredients:**
    - Peel and julienne or grate the carrots.
    - Slice the cucumber, bell pepper, and avocado if using.
    - Wash and dry the spinach or mixed greens.
2. **Assemble the Wraps:**
    - Lay out the tortillas on a flat surface.
    - Spread a generous layer of hummus over each tortilla, leaving a small border around the edges.
    - Arrange the carrots, cucumber, bell pepper, spinach, and any additional vegetables evenly over the hummus.
    - Add avocado slices and red onion if using.
3. **Season:**
    - Sprinkle with salt, pepper, and a squeeze of lemon juice if desired.
4. **Roll the Wraps:**
    - Carefully fold in the sides of the tortilla, then roll it up tightly from the bottom.
5. **Serve:**
    - Cut the wraps in half diagonally and serve immediately, or wrap them in foil or parchment paper for a portable lunch.

Tips:

- **Add Protein:** For extra protein, add some cooked chickpeas, grilled chicken, or feta cheese.
- **Spice it Up:** Add a dash of hot sauce or a sprinkle of your favorite herbs for added flavor.

Enjoy your nutritious and delicious carrot and hummus wraps!

Roasted Veggie Bowl

Ingredients:

For the Roasted Vegetables:

- 1 medium sweet potato, peeled and cubed
- 1 red bell pepper, sliced
- 1 zucchini, sliced
- 1 cup broccoli florets
- 1/2 red onion, sliced
- 2 tbsp olive oil
- 1 tsp paprika
- 1/2 tsp garlic powder
- 1/2 tsp dried oregano (or other herbs of choice)
- Salt and pepper to taste

For the Bowl:

- 1 cup cooked quinoa, brown rice, or couscous
- 1/2 cup hummus or tzatziki (optional)
- Fresh greens (spinach, kale, or arugula)
- 1/4 cup feta cheese or avocado slices (optional)
- Lemon wedges for serving

Instructions:

1. **Preheat Oven:**
   - Preheat your oven to 425°F (220°C).
2. **Prepare the Vegetables:**
   - On a large baking sheet, toss the sweet potato, bell pepper, zucchini, broccoli, and red onion with olive oil, paprika, garlic powder, oregano, salt, and pepper.
3. **Roast the Vegetables:**
   - Spread the vegetables in a single layer on the baking sheet.
   - Roast for 20-25 minutes, or until the vegetables are tender and slightly caramelized, tossing halfway through for even cooking.
4. **Prepare the Base:**
   - While the vegetables are roasting, cook your quinoa, brown rice, or couscous according to package instructions.
5. **Assemble the Bowls:**
   - Divide the cooked base among bowls.
   - Top with roasted vegetables.
   - Add a dollop of hummus or tzatziki if using.
   - Add fresh greens and optional toppings like feta cheese or avocado slices.

6. **Serve:**
    - Garnish with lemon wedges for a fresh squeeze of lemon juice before serving.

Tips:

- **Customization:** Feel free to vary the vegetables based on what you have on hand or seasonal availability.
- **Add Protein:** Include a protein source like grilled chicken, chickpeas, or tofu if desired.
- **Sauces:** Experiment with different sauces like tahini, salsa, or a simple vinaigrette.

Enjoy your vibrant and flavorful roasted veggie bowl!

Quinoa Salad

Ingredients:

- 1 cup quinoa, rinsed
- 2 cups water or vegetable broth
- 1 cup cherry tomatoes, halved
- 1 cucumber, diced
- 1/2 red onion, finely chopped
- 1/2 cup Kalamata olives, pitted and sliced (optional)
- 1/4 cup fresh parsley, chopped (or cilantro)
- 1/4 cup crumbled feta cheese (optional)

For the Dressing:

- 1/4 cup extra-virgin olive oil
- 2 tbsp lemon juice or red wine vinegar
- 1 tsp Dijon mustard
- 1 clove garlic, minced
- 1/2 tsp dried oregano or basil
- Salt and pepper to taste

Instructions:

1. **Cook the Quinoa:**
    - In a medium pot, bring 2 cups of water or vegetable broth to a boil.
    - Add the quinoa, reduce heat to low, cover, and simmer for 15 minutes, or until the quinoa is tender and the liquid is absorbed.
    - Fluff with a fork and let it cool to room temperature.
2. **Prepare the Vegetables:**
    - While the quinoa is cooking, prepare the vegetables and herbs. Chop the tomatoes, cucumber, red onion, and parsley.
3. **Make the Dressing:**
    - In a small bowl or jar, whisk together olive oil, lemon juice (or vinegar), Dijon mustard, minced garlic, dried oregano (or basil), salt, and pepper until well combined.
4. **Combine the Salad:**
    - In a large bowl, combine the cooled quinoa, tomatoes, cucumber, red onion, olives (if using), and parsley.
    - Pour the dressing over the salad and toss to coat all the ingredients.
5. **Add Cheese (Optional):**
    - Gently fold in crumbled feta cheese if desired.
6. **Serve:**

- Serve immediately or chill in the refrigerator for 30 minutes to allow flavors to meld.

Tips:

- **Customization:** Add other ingredients like roasted vegetables, chickpeas, avocado, or nuts for extra flavor and texture.
- **Make-Ahead:** This salad keeps well in the refrigerator for up to 4 days, making it great for meal prep.

Enjoy your fresh and flavorful quinoa salad!

Tomato Basil Soup

Ingredients:

- 2 tbsp olive oil
- 1 medium onion, chopped
- 2 cloves garlic, minced
- 1 (28 oz) can crushed tomatoes (or 4 cups fresh tomatoes, peeled and chopped)
- 1 1/2 cups vegetable or chicken broth
- 1 tsp sugar (optional, to balance acidity)
- 1/2 cup fresh basil leaves, chopped (or 1-2 tbsp dried basil)
- 1/2 cup heavy cream or coconut milk (optional, for creaminess)
- Salt and pepper to taste
- Fresh basil leaves for garnish (optional)
- Grated Parmesan cheese for serving (optional)

Instructions:

1. **Sauté Aromatics:**
    - Heat olive oil in a large pot over medium heat.
    - Add the chopped onion and cook until softened and translucent, about 5 minutes.
    - Stir in the minced garlic and cook for another 1 minute until fragrant.
2. **Add Tomatoes and Broth:**
    - Add the crushed tomatoes to the pot. If using fresh tomatoes, add them along with any juices.
    - Stir in the vegetable or chicken broth.
    - If you like, add a teaspoon of sugar to balance the acidity of the tomatoes.
3. **Simmer:**
    - Bring the mixture to a simmer. Reduce heat and cook for 20-25 minutes to allow flavors to meld.
4. **Blend:**
    - Use an immersion blender to puree the soup directly in the pot until smooth. Alternatively, you can carefully transfer the soup in batches to a countertop blender.
5. **Finish and Season:**
    - Stir in the chopped basil and heavy cream or coconut milk if using. Heat gently until warmed through.
    - Season with salt and pepper to taste.
6. **Serve:**
    - Ladle the soup into bowls. Garnish with fresh basil leaves and a sprinkle of grated Parmesan cheese if desired.

Tips:

- **Roasted Tomatoes:** For deeper flavor, you can roast the tomatoes before adding them to the soup. Simply cut them in half, drizzle with olive oil, and roast at 400°F (200°C) for about 30 minutes.
- **Spice it Up:** Add a pinch of red pepper flakes for a bit of heat or a dash of balsamic vinegar for added depth.

Enjoy your homemade tomato basil soup!

Avocado Toast

Ingredients:

- 2 slices of whole grain or sourdough bread
- 1 ripe avocado
- 1 tbsp lemon juice (or lime juice)
- Salt and pepper to taste
- Optional toppings: cherry tomatoes, radishes, red pepper flakes, fresh herbs, a poached or fried egg, or crumbled feta cheese

Instructions:

1. **Toast the Bread:**
   - Toast the bread slices to your desired level of crispiness.
2. **Prepare the Avocado:**
   - Cut the avocado in half, remove the pit, and scoop the flesh into a bowl.
   - Mash the avocado with a fork, then mix in lemon juice, salt, and pepper to taste.
3. **Assemble the Toast:**
   - Spread the mashed avocado evenly over the toasted bread.
4. **Add Toppings:**
   - Add any optional toppings you like. Some popular choices include sliced cherry tomatoes, radish slices, a sprinkle of red pepper flakes, fresh herbs, a poached or fried egg, or crumbled feta cheese.
5. **Serve:**
   - Serve immediately for the best texture and flavor.

Tips:

- **Variations:** Experiment with different toppings like smoked salmon, pickled onions, or a drizzle of balsamic glaze.
- **Freshness:** If preparing the avocado mash ahead of time, store it with a layer of plastic wrap directly on the surface to prevent browning.

Enjoy your delicious and customizable avocado toast!

Kale and White Bean Stew

Ingredients:

- 1 tbsp olive oil
- 1 medium onion, chopped
- 2 cloves garlic, minced
- 2 carrots, sliced
- 2 celery stalks, chopped
- 1 can (15 oz) white beans (cannellini or great northern), drained and rinsed
- 1 can (14.5 oz) diced tomatoes
- 4 cups vegetable or chicken broth
- 1 bunch kale, stems removed and leaves chopped
- 1 tsp dried thyme
- 1/2 tsp dried rosemary
- 1 bay leaf
- Salt and pepper to taste
- Optional: 1 cup chopped potatoes or sweet potatoes for added heartiness

Instructions:

1. **Sauté Aromatics:**
   - Heat olive oil in a large pot over medium heat.
   - Add the chopped onion, carrots, and celery. Cook until softened, about 5-7 minutes.
   - Stir in the minced garlic and cook for another 1 minute until fragrant.
2. **Add Vegetables and Beans:**
   - Add the diced tomatoes (with their juice), white beans, and optional potatoes or sweet potatoes if using.
3. **Add Broth and Seasonings:**
   - Pour in the vegetable or chicken broth.
   - Stir in thyme, rosemary, bay leaf, salt, and pepper.
4. **Simmer:**
   - Bring to a boil, then reduce heat and let simmer for 15-20 minutes, or until vegetables are tender.
5. **Add Kale:**
   - Stir in the chopped kale and cook for an additional 5-7 minutes until the kale is wilted and tender.
6. **Serve:**
   - Remove the bay leaf before serving. Adjust seasoning with more salt and pepper if needed.

Tips:

- **Make Ahead:** This stew can be made ahead and stored in the refrigerator for up to 4 days or frozen for up to 3 months.
- **Flavor Boost:** For extra flavor, add a splash of balsamic vinegar or a sprinkle of Parmesan cheese before serving.

Enjoy your warming kale and white bean stew!

Stuffed Acorn Squash

1. **Ingredients:**
    1. 2 acorn squashes
    2. 1 cup quinoa or rice (cooked)
    3. 1 cup cooked and crumbled sausage (optional)
    4. 1/2 cup chopped nuts (like walnuts or pecans)
    5. 1/2 cup dried cranberries or raisins
    6. 1 small onion (diced)
    7. 2 cloves garlic (minced)
    8. 1 tsp dried thyme
    9. 1 tsp dried sage
    10. Olive oil
    11. Salt and pepper to taste
2. **Instructions:**
    1. Preheat oven to 400°F (200°C).
    2. Halve the acorn squashes and scoop out seeds.
    3. Brush the inside with olive oil, season with salt and pepper, and place cut-side down on a baking sheet. Roast for 25-30 minutes.
    4. In a pan, sauté onion and garlic in olive oil until softened. Add sausage (if using), nuts, cranberries, thyme, and sage. Stir in cooked quinoa or rice. Season to taste.
    5. Fill roasted squashes with the mixture and return to the oven. Bake for an additional 10-15 minutes until everything is heated through.

Enjoy your ultimate stuffed acorn squash!

Veggie Sushi Rolls

Ingredients:

- **For the Sushi Rice:**
    - 1 cup sushi rice
    - 1 1/4 cups water
    - 2 tbsp rice vinegar
    - 1 tbsp sugar
    - 1/2 tsp salt
- **For the Filling:**
    - 1 cucumber, julienned
    - 1 carrot, julienned
    - 1 avocado, sliced
    - 1 bell pepper (any color), julienned
    - 1 small zucchini, julienned (optional)
- **For Assembly:**
    - Nori sheets (seaweed)
    - Soy sauce (for dipping)
    - Pickled ginger (optional)
    - Wasabi (optional)

Instructions:

1. **Prepare the Sushi Rice:**
    1. Rinse the sushi rice under cold water until the water runs clear. This helps remove excess starch.
    2. Combine the rinsed rice and water in a rice cooker or pot. Cook according to the rice cooker's instructions or bring to a boil, reduce heat, cover, and simmer for about 20 minutes until the water is absorbed.
    3. While the rice is cooking, mix the rice vinegar, sugar, and salt in a small bowl until dissolved.
    4. Once the rice is cooked, transfer it to a large bowl and gently fold in the vinegar mixture. Allow the rice to cool to room temperature.
2. **Prepare the Vegetables:**
    1. Wash and julienne the cucumber, carrot, bell pepper, and zucchini.
    2. Slice the avocado.
3. **Assemble the Sushi Rolls:**
    1. Place a sheet of nori on a bamboo sushi mat, shiny side down.
    2. Wet your hands (to prevent sticking) and spread a thin, even layer of sushi rice over the nori, leaving about 1 inch of nori at the top edge.
    3. Lay the vegetables in a line along the bottom edge of the rice.

4. Using the bamboo mat, carefully roll the sushi away from you, pressing gently to keep the roll tight. Seal the edge of the nori with a little water.

4. **Slice and Serve:**
   1. Using a sharp knife, slice the roll into bite-sized pieces. Clean the knife between cuts to prevent sticking.
   2. Arrange the sushi rolls on a plate. Serve with soy sauce, pickled ginger, and wasabi if desired.

Enjoy your homemade veggie sushi rolls!

Sweet Potato Fries

Ingredients:

- 2 large sweet potatoes
- 2 tbsp olive oil
- 1 tsp paprika
- 1/2 tsp garlic powder
- 1/2 tsp onion powder
- 1/2 tsp ground cumin
- Salt and pepper to taste

Instructions:

1. **Preheat Oven:** Preheat your oven to 425°F (220°C).
2. **Prepare Sweet Potatoes:** Peel the sweet potatoes and cut them into fries or wedges.
3. **Season:** In a large bowl, toss the sweet potato fries with olive oil, paprika, garlic powder, onion powder, cumin, salt, and pepper.
4. **Bake:** Spread the fries in a single layer on a baking sheet lined with parchment paper. Bake for 25-30 minutes, flipping halfway through, until they are crispy and golden brown.
5. **Serve:** Let cool slightly before serving. Enjoy with your favorite dipping sauce!

These sweet potato fries are an ultimate treat with their crispy exterior and soft interior.

Creamy Tomato Pasta

Ingredients:

- **For the Pasta:**
    - 12 oz (340 g) pasta (penne, fettuccine, or your choice)
    - Salt (for pasta water)
- **For the Sauce:**
    - 2 tbsp olive oil
    - 1 small onion, finely chopped
    - 2 cloves garlic, minced
    - 1 can (14.5 oz) crushed tomatoes
    - 1/2 cup heavy cream (or half-and-half for a lighter version)
    - 1/4 cup tomato paste
    - 1 tsp dried basil
    - 1/2 tsp dried oregano
    - 1/4 tsp red pepper flakes (optional, for heat)
    - Salt and black pepper to taste
    - Fresh basil or parsley for garnish (optional)
    - Grated Parmesan cheese (optional)

Instructions:

1. **Cook the Pasta:**
    - Bring a large pot of salted water to a boil.
    - Cook the pasta according to the package instructions until al dente. Drain and set aside.
2. **Prepare the Sauce:**
    - Heat the olive oil in a large skillet over medium heat.
    - Add the chopped onion and cook until softened and translucent, about 3-4 minutes.
    - Add the minced garlic and cook for an additional 30 seconds, until fragrant.
    - Stir in the crushed tomatoes, tomato paste, dried basil, oregano, and red pepper flakes (if using). Simmer for about 5 minutes.
    - Reduce the heat to low and slowly stir in the heavy cream. Let the sauce simmer for another 3-5 minutes, stirring occasionally. Season with salt and black pepper to taste.
3. **Combine:**
    - Add the cooked pasta to the sauce and toss to coat, allowing the pasta to soak up the creamy tomato sauce.
4. **Serve:**
    - Garnish with fresh basil or parsley and a sprinkle of grated Parmesan cheese if desired.

Enjoy your creamy tomato pasta! It's a classic dish that's perfect for a quick weeknight dinner or a comforting meal anytime.

Vegetable Curry

Ingredients:

- **For the Curry:**
    - 2 tbsp vegetable oil
    - 1 large onion, finely chopped
    - 3 cloves garlic, minced
    - 1 tbsp fresh ginger, minced
    - 2 tbsp curry powder (adjust to taste)
    - 1 tsp ground cumin
    - 1 tsp ground coriander
    - 1/2 tsp turmeric
    - 1/2 tsp paprika
    - 1 can (14.5 oz) diced tomatoes
    - 1 cup coconut milk
    - 1 cup vegetable broth
    - 2 cups mixed vegetables (e.g., carrots, bell peppers, potatoes, peas, cauliflower, green beans)
    - 1 cup chickpeas (canned or cooked)
    - Salt and black pepper to taste
    - Fresh cilantro for garnish (optional)
- **For Serving:**
    - Cooked rice or naan bread

Instructions:

1. **Prepare the Vegetables:**
    - Wash and cut the vegetables into bite-sized pieces. If using potatoes or carrots, consider pre-cooking them a bit to ensure they cook evenly with the other veggies.
2. **Sauté Aromatics:**
    - Heat the vegetable oil in a large skillet or pot over medium heat.
    - Add the chopped onion and cook until softened and translucent, about 5 minutes.
    - Add the garlic and ginger, cooking for another 1-2 minutes until fragrant.
3. **Add Spices:**
    - Stir in the curry powder, cumin, coriander, turmeric, and paprika. Cook for another minute, allowing the spices to toast and release their flavors.
4. **Add Tomatoes and Liquids:**
    - Stir in the diced tomatoes, coconut milk, and vegetable broth. Bring the mixture to a simmer.
5. **Cook Vegetables:**

- Add the mixed vegetables and chickpeas. Stir well and let the curry simmer for about 15-20 minutes, or until the vegetables are tender and cooked through. If the curry gets too thick, add a bit more vegetable broth or water to reach your desired consistency.
6. **Season and Garnish:**
    - Season with salt and black pepper to taste. Garnish with fresh cilantro if desired.
7. **Serve:**
    - Serve the vegetable curry over cooked rice or with naan bread for a complete meal.

This vegetable curry is versatile, so feel free to adjust the vegetables and spices to your taste preferences. Enjoy your comforting and aromatic curry!

Beet Salad

Ingredients:

- **For the Salad:**
    - 4 medium beets (red or golden)
    - 4 cups mixed greens (e.g., arugula, spinach, or baby kale)
    - 1/2 cup crumbled feta cheese or goat cheese
    - 1/4 cup toasted walnuts or pecans (optional)
    - 1/4 cup thinly sliced red onion
    - 1/4 cup fresh parsley or basil, chopped (optional)
- **For the Dressing:**
    - 3 tbsp olive oil
    - 2 tbsp balsamic vinegar or red wine vinegar
    - 1 tbsp Dijon mustard
    - 1 tsp honey or maple syrup (optional for sweetness)
    - 1 clove garlic, minced
    - Salt and black pepper to taste

Instructions:

1. **Prepare the Beets:**
    - Preheat your oven to 400°F (200°C).
    - Wash and trim the beets. Place them on a baking sheet and drizzle with olive oil. Wrap each beet individually in aluminum foil.
    - Roast in the preheated oven for about 45-60 minutes, or until the beets are tender when pierced with a fork. Allow them to cool slightly.
    - Once cool, peel the beets (the skins should come off easily) and cut them into bite-sized cubes.
2. **Prepare the Dressing:**
    - In a small bowl or jar, whisk together the olive oil, vinegar, Dijon mustard, honey (if using), minced garlic, salt, and black pepper until well combined.
3. **Assemble the Salad:**
    - In a large bowl, toss the mixed greens with a little of the dressing.
    - Add the roasted beet cubes, crumbled cheese, toasted nuts, and sliced red onion.
    - Drizzle with more dressing and toss gently to combine.
4. **Garnish and Serve:**
    - Garnish with fresh parsley or basil if desired.
    - Serve immediately or chill for a bit if you prefer a colder salad.

This beet salad is wonderfully colorful and packed with flavors. The sweetness of the roasted beets pairs beautifully with the tangy dressing and creamy cheese. Enjoy!

Portobello Mushroom Tacos

Ingredients:

- **For the Tacos:**
    - 4 large Portobello mushrooms
    - 2 tbsp olive oil
    - 1 tbsp soy sauce or tamari
    - 1 tsp smoked paprika
    - 1/2 tsp ground cumin
    - 1/2 tsp garlic powder
    - 1/4 tsp chili powder (optional, for heat)
    - Salt and black pepper to taste
    - 8 small corn or flour tortillas
- **For the Toppings:**
    - 1 cup shredded cabbage or lettuce
    - 1 avocado, sliced
    - 1/4 cup chopped cilantro
    - Lime wedges
    - Salsa or pico de gallo (optional)
    - Crumbled feta or cotija cheese (optional)

Instructions:

1. **Prepare the Mushrooms:**
    - Clean the Portobello mushrooms and remove the stems. Slice them into strips.
    - In a bowl, mix olive oil, soy sauce, smoked paprika, cumin, garlic powder, chili powder, salt, and pepper.
    - Toss the mushroom strips in the marinade until well coated.
2. **Cook the Mushrooms:**
    - Heat a skillet over medium-high heat. Add the mushrooms and cook for about 5-7 minutes, stirring occasionally, until they are tender and slightly crispy on the edges.
3. **Warm the Tortillas:**
    - Heat the tortillas in a dry skillet over medium heat for about 30 seconds per side, or until warm and pliable.
4. **Assemble the Tacos:**
    - Place a few mushroom strips on each tortilla.
    - Top with shredded cabbage or lettuce, avocado slices, and chopped cilantro.
    - Add a squeeze of lime juice and any additional toppings like salsa or crumbled cheese if desired.

These Portobello mushroom tacos are packed with umami flavor and make a satisfying meatless option. Enjoy your flavorful and hearty tacos!

Corn and Black Bean Salad

Ingredients:

- **For the Salad:**
    - 1 can (15 oz) black beans, drained and rinsed
    - 2 cups corn kernels (fresh, frozen, or canned)
    - 1 red bell pepper, diced
    - 1/2 red onion, finely chopped
    - 1/2 cup cherry tomatoes, halved
    - 1/4 cup chopped fresh cilantro
    - 1 avocado, diced (optional)
- **For the Dressing:**
    - 3 tbsp olive oil
    - 2 tbsp lime juice
    - 1 tbsp red wine vinegar
    - 1 tsp ground cumin
    - 1/2 tsp garlic powder
    - Salt and black pepper to taste

Instructions:

1. **Prepare the Vegetables:**
    - If using frozen corn, cook according to package instructions and let it cool. If using fresh corn, you can roast or boil it briefly.
2. **Mix the Salad:**
    - In a large bowl, combine the black beans, corn, red bell pepper, red onion, cherry tomatoes, and cilantro. Add the diced avocado if using.
3. **Prepare the Dressing:**
    - In a small bowl, whisk together olive oil, lime juice, red wine vinegar, ground cumin, garlic powder, salt, and pepper.
4. **Combine and Serve:**
    - Pour the dressing over the salad and toss gently to coat. Adjust seasoning if needed.

This corn and black bean salad is perfect as a side dish or light main course. Enjoy its vibrant flavors and textures!

Vegan Burritos

Ingredients:

- **For the Burritos:**
    - 1 tbsp olive oil
    - 1 small onion, diced
    - 2 cloves garlic, minced
    - 1 bell pepper, diced
    - 1 cup cooked black beans (or 1 can, drained and rinsed)
    - 1 cup cooked corn kernels (fresh, frozen, or canned)
    - 1 cup cooked rice (white, brown, or your choice)
    - 1 cup diced tomatoes (fresh or canned)
    - 1 tsp ground cumin
    - 1/2 tsp smoked paprika
    - 1/2 tsp chili powder (optional, for heat)
    - Salt and black pepper to taste
    - 4 large tortillas (flour or whole wheat)
- **For the Optional Add-ins and Toppings:**
    - 1 avocado, sliced or mashed
    - 1/2 cup salsa or pico de gallo
    - 1/2 cup chopped fresh cilantro
    - Lime wedges
    - Vegan cheese or cashew cream (optional)
    - Shredded lettuce or spinach (optional)

Instructions:

1. **Cook the Vegetables:**
    - Heat olive oil in a large skillet over medium heat.
    - Add the diced onion and cook until softened, about 3-4 minutes.
    - Stir in the minced garlic and cook for another 30 seconds.
2. **Add the Beans and Corn:**
    - Add the bell pepper, black beans, corn, and cooked rice to the skillet.
    - Stir in the diced tomatoes, ground cumin, smoked paprika, chili powder (if using), salt, and black pepper.
    - Cook for about 5-7 minutes, stirring occasionally, until everything is heated through and the flavors are well combined.
3. **Warm the Tortillas:**
    - Heat the tortillas in a dry skillet over medium heat for about 30 seconds per side, or until warm and pliable. You can also wrap them in foil and warm them in the oven.
4. **Assemble the Burritos:**

- Lay out a tortilla on a flat surface.
- Spoon a portion of the filling onto the center of the tortilla.
- Add any optional toppings like avocado slices, salsa, cilantro, or vegan cheese.
- Fold the sides of the tortilla over the filling, then roll up from the bottom to form a burrito.

5. **Serve:**
    - Serve the burritos immediately with lime wedges on the side. You can also toast them in a skillet for a few minutes on each side if you like them crispy.

These vegan burritos are versatile, so feel free to add or substitute ingredients based on your preferences. Enjoy your hearty and delicious meal!

Green Smoothie Bowl

Ingredients:

- **For the Smoothie Base:**
    - 1 cup fresh spinach or kale
    - 1 banana, sliced (preferably frozen)
    - 1/2 cup frozen pineapple chunks
    - 1/2 cup frozen mango chunks
    - 1/2 cup unsweetened almond milk (or any plant-based milk)
    - 1 tbsp chia seeds or flaxseeds (optional)
- **For Toppings:**
    - 1/4 cup granola
    - 1/4 cup sliced fresh fruit (e.g., kiwi, berries, banana)
    - 1 tbsp hemp seeds or nuts
    - A drizzle of honey or maple syrup (optional)
    - Coconut flakes (optional)

Instructions:

1. **Blend the Smoothie:**
    - In a blender, combine the spinach or kale, frozen banana, pineapple, mango, almond milk, and chia seeds if using.
    - Blend until smooth and creamy. If needed, add a little more almond milk to reach your desired consistency.
2. **Serve:**
    - Pour the smoothie into a bowl.
3. **Add Toppings:**
    - Arrange your desired toppings on top of the smoothie. Be creative and use a variety of textures and flavors.
4. **Enjoy:**
    - Serve immediately for the freshest taste and enjoy your nutritious green smoothie bowl!

This bowl is packed with vitamins and minerals, making it a great way to start your day or enjoy as a refreshing snack.

Ratatouille

Ingredients:

- **For the Ratatouille:**
    - 2 tbsp olive oil
    - 1 large onion, diced
    - 3 cloves garlic, minced
    - 1 red bell pepper, diced
    - 1 yellow bell pepper, diced
    - 1 medium eggplant, diced
    - 2 medium zucchini, diced
    - 1 cup cherry tomatoes or 1 can (14.5 oz) diced tomatoes
    - 1 tbsp tomato paste
    - 1 tsp dried basil
    - 1 tsp dried thyme
    - 1/2 tsp dried oregano
    - 1/4 tsp red pepper flakes (optional, for heat)
    - Salt and black pepper to taste
    - Fresh basil or parsley for garnish (optional)

Instructions:

1. **Sauté Aromatics:**
    - Heat olive oil in a large skillet or Dutch oven over medium heat.
    - Add the diced onion and cook until softened and translucent, about 5 minutes.
    - Stir in the minced garlic and cook for an additional 1 minute until fragrant.
2. **Cook Vegetables:**
    - Add the diced bell peppers to the skillet and cook for about 5 minutes, until they start to soften.
    - Add the diced eggplant and zucchini. Cook, stirring occasionally, for about 10 minutes, until the vegetables are tender and starting to brown.
3. **Add Tomatoes and Seasonings:**
    - Stir in the cherry tomatoes or canned diced tomatoes, tomato paste, dried basil, thyme, oregano, and red pepper flakes if using.
    - Season with salt and black pepper to taste.
4. **Simmer:**
    - Reduce the heat to low, cover, and let the ratatouille simmer for about 20-25 minutes, stirring occasionally. The flavors should meld together and the vegetables should be tender.
5. **Serve:**
    - Garnish with fresh basil or parsley if desired. Serve hot, warm, or at room temperature.

Serving Suggestions:

- Ratatouille can be served on its own or with crusty bread.
- It pairs beautifully with rice, quinoa, or pasta.
- You can also serve it alongside grilled meats or as a topping for polenta.

Enjoy this vibrant and wholesome vegetable dish!

Spaghetti Squash Primavera

Ingredients:

- **For the Spaghetti Squash:**
    - 1 large spaghetti squash
    - 2 tbsp olive oil
    - Salt and black pepper to taste
- **For the Primavera Sauce:**
    - 2 tbsp olive oil
    - 1 small onion, diced
    - 2 cloves garlic, minced
    - 1 red bell pepper, diced
    - 1 yellow bell pepper, diced
    - 1 medium zucchini, diced
    - 1 cup cherry tomatoes, halved
    - 1/2 cup frozen peas (optional)
    - 1 tsp dried basil
    - 1/2 tsp dried oregano
    - 1/4 tsp red pepper flakes (optional, for heat)
    - Salt and black pepper to taste
    - 1/4 cup grated Parmesan cheese or nutritional yeast (for a vegan option)
- **For Garnish (optional):**
    - Fresh basil or parsley, chopped
    - Extra grated Parmesan cheese or nutritional yeast

Instructions:

1. **Prepare the Spaghetti Squash:**
    - Preheat your oven to 400°F (200°C).
    - Cut the spaghetti squash in half lengthwise and scoop out the seeds.
    - Brush the inside of each half with olive oil and season with salt and pepper.
    - Place the squash halves cut-side down on a baking sheet lined with parchment paper.
    - Roast in the preheated oven for 35-45 minutes, or until the flesh is tender and can be easily shredded with a fork. Let cool slightly.
2. **Prepare the Primavera Sauce:**
    - While the squash is roasting, heat olive oil in a large skillet over medium heat.
    - Add the diced onion and cook until softened and translucent, about 5 minutes.
    - Stir in the minced garlic and cook for another 1 minute until fragrant.
    - Add the bell peppers, zucchini, and cherry tomatoes. Cook for about 5-7 minutes, until the vegetables are tender.

- Stir in the peas (if using), dried basil, oregano, red pepper flakes (if using), salt, and black pepper. Cook for another 2-3 minutes, until the peas are heated through and the flavors are well combined.
3. **Combine and Serve:**
    - Once the spaghetti squash is cool enough to handle, use a fork to scrape the flesh into strands.
    - Gently toss the spaghetti squash strands with the primavera sauce in the skillet.
    - Sprinkle with grated Parmesan cheese or nutritional yeast.
    - Garnish with fresh basil or parsley if desired.

Serving Suggestions:

- Serve the Spaghetti Squash Primavera hot as a main dish or as a side.
- You can also add cooked chicken, shrimp, or tofu for added protein.

Enjoy this light, flavorful, and veggie-packed meal!

Lentil Loaf

Ingredients:

- **For the Lentil Mixture:**
    - 1 cup dried green or brown lentils
    - 2 1/2 cups water or vegetable broth
    - 1 tbsp olive oil
    - 1 small onion, diced
    - 2 cloves garlic, minced
    - 1 cup grated carrots
    - 1 cup finely chopped mushrooms
    - 1/2 cup rolled oats
    - 1/4 cup ground flaxseed (or 2 tbsp flaxseed meal)
    - 2 tbsp tomato paste
    - 2 tbsp soy sauce or tamari
    - 1 tsp dried thyme
    - 1/2 tsp dried rosemary
    - 1/2 tsp smoked paprika
    - Salt and black pepper to taste
- **For the Topping:**
    - 1/4 cup ketchup or barbecue sauce

Instructions:

1. **Cook the Lentils:**
    - Rinse the lentils under cold water. In a medium saucepan, combine lentils and water or broth. Bring to a boil, then reduce heat and simmer for about 25-30 minutes, or until lentils are tender. Drain any excess liquid and let cool slightly.
2. **Prepare the Veggies:**
    - While the lentils are cooking, heat olive oil in a large skillet over medium heat.
    - Add the diced onion and cook until softened, about 5 minutes.
    - Stir in the minced garlic, grated carrots, and chopped mushrooms. Cook for another 5-7 minutes until the vegetables are tender and the mushrooms have released their moisture.
3. **Combine Ingredients:**
    - In a large bowl, mash the cooked lentils with a fork or potato masher, leaving some texture.
    - Add the cooked vegetables, rolled oats, ground flaxseed, tomato paste, soy sauce, dried thyme, rosemary, smoked paprika, salt, and pepper. Mix until well combined.
4. **Bake the Loaf:**

- Preheat your oven to 375°F (190°C). Line a loaf pan with parchment paper or lightly grease it.
- Press the lentil mixture evenly into the loaf pan.
- Spread ketchup or barbecue sauce on top.

5. **Cook:**
   - Bake for 40-45 minutes, or until the loaf is firm and the top is slightly caramelized.
   - Let it cool in the pan for about 10 minutes before slicing.

Serving Suggestions:

- Serve the lentil loaf with mashed potatoes, a side salad, or steamed vegetables.
- It's also great with a side of vegan gravy or your favorite sauce.

Enjoy this comforting and nutritious lentil loaf!

Roasted Brussels Sprouts

Ingredients:

- 1 lb (450 g) Brussels sprouts
- 2 tbsp olive oil
- 1/2 tsp salt
- 1/4 tsp black pepper
- 1/2 tsp garlic powder (optional)
- 1/2 tsp smoked paprika (optional)
- 1 tbsp balsamic vinegar (optional, for extra flavor)
- 2 tbsp grated Parmesan cheese or nutritional yeast (optional, for a vegan option)

Instructions:

1. **Preheat the Oven:**
   - Preheat your oven to 425°F (220°C).
2. **Prepare the Brussels Sprouts:**
   - Trim the ends off the Brussels sprouts and remove any yellow or damaged leaves.
   - Cut the Brussels sprouts in half lengthwise to ensure even roasting.
3. **Season:**
   - In a large bowl, toss the halved Brussels sprouts with olive oil, salt, pepper, garlic powder, and smoked paprika if using.
4. **Roast:**
   - Spread the Brussels sprouts in a single layer on a baking sheet. Make sure they are not overcrowded to allow for even roasting.
   - Roast in the preheated oven for 20-25 minutes, or until the Brussels sprouts are golden brown and crispy on the edges. Shake the pan or stir the sprouts halfway through cooking for even browning.
5. **Finish (optional):**
   - If you like, drizzle with balsamic vinegar and toss to coat right after roasting.
   - Sprinkle with grated Parmesan cheese or nutritional yeast if desired.
6. **Serve:**
   - Serve hot as a side dish or snack.

Tips:

- For extra crispiness, you can cut the Brussels sprouts into smaller pieces or increase the roasting time slightly, but watch them closely to avoid burning.
- Add a sprinkle of red pepper flakes for a bit of heat, or toss with a bit of lemon zest for a fresh touch.

Enjoy these roasted Brussels sprouts as a delicious and healthy addition to any meal!

Veggie Wraps

Ingredients:

- **For the Wraps:**
    - 4 large whole wheat or flour tortillas
    - 1 cup hummus (store-bought or homemade)
    - 1 cup mixed greens (e.g., spinach, arugula)
    - 1 red bell pepper, sliced
    - 1 cucumber, sliced
    - 1 large carrot, julienned
    - 1 avocado, sliced
    - 1/4 cup red onion, thinly sliced
    - 1/4 cup crumbled feta cheese or vegan cheese (optional)
    - 1/4 cup fresh herbs (e.g., cilantro, basil) (optional)
- **For the Dressing (optional):**
    - 2 tbsp olive oil
    - 1 tbsp lemon juice or apple cider vinegar
    - 1 tsp Dijon mustard
    - Salt and black pepper to taste

Instructions:

1. **Prepare the Veggies:**
    - Wash and slice all your vegetables as needed.
2. **Prepare the Dressing (if using):**
    - In a small bowl, whisk together olive oil, lemon juice, Dijon mustard, salt, and pepper.
3. **Assemble the Wraps:**
    - Lay out the tortillas on a flat surface.
    - Spread a generous layer of hummus over each tortilla.
    - Layer the mixed greens, bell pepper, cucumber, carrot, avocado, and red onion evenly on top of the hummus.
    - Sprinkle with crumbled feta cheese and fresh herbs if using.
4. **Roll the Wraps:**
    - Fold in the sides of the tortilla, then roll it up tightly from the bottom to enclose the filling.
5. **Serve:**
    - Slice the wraps in half diagonally if desired.
    - Drizzle with the optional dressing before serving or serve it on the side.

Tips:

- Feel free to add other veggies or proteins like grilled chicken, tofu, or chickpeas.
- You can also use different spreads like guacamole, tzatziki, or a yogurt-based dressing.

These veggie wraps are perfect for a quick lunch, a light dinner, or a healthy snack!

Thai Peanut Noodles

Ingredients:

- **For the Noodles:**
    - 8 oz (225 g) rice noodles or soba noodles
    - 1 tbsp vegetable oil
    - 1 red bell pepper, sliced
    - 1 cup snap peas or snow peas
    - 1 medium carrot, julienned
    - 1 cup shredded cabbage (optional)
    - 2 green onions, sliced
    - 1/4 cup chopped peanuts (optional, for garnish)
    - Fresh cilantro or basil, for garnish
- **For the Peanut Sauce:**
    - 1/4 cup creamy peanut butter
    - 3 tbsp soy sauce or tamari
    - 2 tbsp rice vinegar or lime juice
    - 2 tbsp honey or maple syrup
    - 1 tbsp sesame oil
    - 1-2 tbsp water (to thin the sauce)
    - 1 clove garlic, minced
    - 1 tsp freshly grated ginger
    - 1/2 tsp red pepper flakes or sriracha (optional, for heat)

Instructions:

1. **Cook the Noodles:**
    - Cook the rice noodles or soba noodles according to the package instructions. Drain and rinse under cold water to stop cooking and prevent sticking.
2. **Prepare the Peanut Sauce:**
    - In a medium bowl, whisk together the peanut butter, soy sauce, rice vinegar or lime juice, honey or maple syrup, sesame oil, garlic, ginger, and red pepper flakes or sriracha (if using). If the sauce is too thick, add water a tablespoon at a time until you reach your desired consistency.
3. **Cook the Vegetables:**
    - Heat vegetable oil in a large skillet or wok over medium-high heat.
    - Add the bell pepper, snap peas, and carrot. Stir-fry for about 3-5 minutes, until the vegetables are tender-crisp.
    - If using cabbage, add it in the last 1-2 minutes of cooking.
4. **Combine Noodles and Sauce:**
    - Add the cooked noodles to the skillet with the vegetables. Pour the peanut sauce over the noodles and vegetables.

- Toss everything together until well coated and heated through.
5. **Garnish and Serve:**
    - Transfer the noodles to serving bowls.
    - Garnish with chopped peanuts, sliced green onions, and fresh cilantro or basil.

Tips:

- Feel free to add protein like grilled chicken, tofu, or shrimp for a more substantial meal.
- Adjust the spiciness of the peanut sauce to your taste by adding more or less red pepper flakes or sriracha.

Enjoy these delicious Thai Peanut Noodles for a satisfying and flavorful meal!

Falafel

Ingredients:

- **For the Falafel:**
    - 1 cup dried chickpeas (not canned)
    - 1 small onion, roughly chopped
    - 2 cloves garlic, minced
    - 1/2 cup fresh parsley, chopped
    - 1/2 cup fresh cilantro, chopped
    - 1 tsp ground cumin
    - 1 tsp ground coriander
    - 1/2 tsp baking powder
    - 1/2 tsp salt
    - 1/4 tsp black pepper
    - 2-3 tbsp flour (all-purpose or chickpea flour)
    - Vegetable oil, for frying
- **For Serving (optional):**
    - Pita bread or flatbread
    - Hummus or tahini sauce
    - Shredded lettuce
    - Sliced tomatoes
    - Sliced cucumbers
    - Pickles

Instructions:

1. **Soak the Chickpeas:**
    - Place dried chickpeas in a large bowl and cover with water. Soak overnight, or for at least 8 hours. Drain well.
2. **Prepare the Mixture:**
    - In a food processor, combine soaked and drained chickpeas, onion, garlic, parsley, cilantro, cumin, coriander, baking powder, salt, and pepper.
    - Process until the mixture is finely ground but still slightly coarse. Scrape down the sides of the bowl as needed.
    - If the mixture is too wet, add flour a tablespoon at a time until it holds together when shaped.
3. **Form the Falafel:**
    - With wet hands or using a falafel scoop, form the mixture into 1-inch balls or patties.
4. **Fry the Falafel:**
    - Heat 2-3 inches of vegetable oil in a deep skillet or pan over medium-high heat until it reaches 350°F (175°C).

- Carefully drop the falafel balls into the hot oil, working in batches to avoid overcrowding. Fry for 3-4 minutes, or until golden brown and crispy.
- Use a slotted spoon to remove falafel from the oil and drain on paper towels.

5. **Serve:**
    - Serve falafel warm with pita bread, hummus, tahini sauce, and your choice of fresh veggies and pickles.

Tips:

- If you prefer baking, place falafel on a baking sheet lined with parchment paper, brush lightly with oil, and bake at 375°F (190°C) for 20-25 minutes, turning halfway through.
- For a smoother texture, you can blend the mixture a bit longer, but be careful not to over-process.

Enjoy your homemade falafel as a delicious and versatile dish!

Sweet Potato and Black Bean Enchiladas

Ingredients:

- **For the Enchiladas:**
    - 2 medium sweet potatoes, peeled and diced
    - 1 tbsp olive oil
    - 1 small onion, diced
    - 2 cloves garlic, minced
    - 1 can (15 oz) black beans, drained and rinsed
    - 1 cup corn kernels (fresh, frozen, or canned)
    - 1 cup shredded cheese (cheddar, Monterey Jack, or vegan cheese) (optional)
    - 8-10 corn or flour tortillas
- **For the Enchilada Sauce:**
    - 2 tbsp olive oil
    - 2 tbsp all-purpose flour
    - 2 tbsp chili powder
    - 1 tsp ground cumin
    - 1/2 tsp smoked paprika
    - 1/4 tsp garlic powder
    - 1/4 tsp onion powder
    - 1 can (15 oz) tomato sauce
    - 1 cup vegetable broth
    - Salt and black pepper to taste
- **For Garnish (optional):**
    - Fresh cilantro, chopped
    - Sliced avocado
    - Lime wedges
    - Sour cream or Greek yogurt

Instructions:

1. **Prepare the Sweet Potatoes:**
    - Preheat your oven to 400°F (200°C).
    - Toss the diced sweet potatoes with olive oil, salt, and pepper. Spread them on a baking sheet in a single layer.
    - Roast for 20-25 minutes, or until tender and slightly caramelized, stirring halfway through.
2. **Make the Enchilada Sauce:**
    - In a saucepan, heat olive oil over medium heat.
    - Whisk in flour and cook for 1 minute until lightly golden.
    - Add chili powder, cumin, smoked paprika, garlic powder, and onion powder. Cook for another 30 seconds.

- Gradually whisk in tomato sauce and vegetable broth. Bring to a simmer and cook for about 5 minutes, until slightly thickened. Season with salt and pepper.

3. **Prepare the Filling:**
    - In a large skillet, heat a little olive oil over medium heat. Sauté the onion until softened, about 5 minutes.
    - Stir in the garlic and cook for another minute.
    - Add the roasted sweet potatoes, black beans, and corn. Cook until everything is heated through and well combined. Adjust seasoning with salt and pepper if needed.

4. **Assemble the Enchiladas:**
    - Preheat your oven to 375°F (190°C).
    - Spread a small amount of enchilada sauce on the bottom of a baking dish.
    - Fill each tortilla with the sweet potato and black bean mixture. Optionally, sprinkle some shredded cheese over the filling.
    - Roll up the tortillas and place them seam-side down in the baking dish.
    - Pour the remaining enchilada sauce over the rolled tortillas and sprinkle with additional cheese if desired.

5. **Bake:**
    - Cover the baking dish with foil and bake for 20 minutes.
    - Remove the foil and bake for an additional 10 minutes, or until the cheese is melted and bubbly.

6. **Serve:**
    - Garnish with chopped cilantro, sliced avocado, lime wedges, and a dollop of sour cream or Greek yogurt if desired.

Enjoy these delicious and satisfying sweet potato and black bean enchiladas!

Cauliflower Steaks

Ingredients:

- 1 large cauliflower
- 3 tbsp olive oil
- 1 tsp smoked paprika
- 1 tsp garlic powder
- 1/2 tsp ground cumin
- 1/2 tsp ground turmeric (optional, for color)
- Salt and black pepper to taste
- 2 tbsp fresh lemon juice or balsamic vinegar (optional, for finishing)
- Fresh herbs for garnish (e.g., parsley, cilantro)

Instructions:

1. **Prepare the Cauliflower:**
   - Preheat your oven to 425°F (220°C).
   - Remove the leaves from the cauliflower and trim the stem so that the head sits flat on the cutting board.
   - Slice the cauliflower into 1/2-inch to 1-inch thick "steaks" from the center of the cauliflower. You should be able to get 2-4 steaks from one large head, depending on its size. Some florets may fall off; you can roast these as well.
2. **Season the Steaks:**
   - Place the cauliflower steaks and any loose florets on a baking sheet.
   - Brush both sides of the cauliflower steaks with olive oil.
   - In a small bowl, mix the smoked paprika, garlic powder, cumin, turmeric (if using), salt, and black pepper.
   - Sprinkle the spice mixture evenly over both sides of the cauliflower steaks.
3. **Roast the Cauliflower:**
   - Roast in the preheated oven for 20-25 minutes, flipping the steaks halfway through, until the cauliflower is tender and golden brown on the edges.
4. **Finish and Serve:**
   - Remove from the oven and drizzle with fresh lemon juice or balsamic vinegar if desired.
   - Garnish with fresh herbs like parsley or cilantro.

Serving Suggestions:

- **As a Main Dish:** Serve with a side of quinoa, rice, or a grain salad.
- **As a Side:** Pair with grilled meats or a hearty salad.
- **With Sauces:** Top with tahini sauce, yogurt sauce, or a drizzle of your favorite dressing.

Tips:

- If you want extra crispy edges, you can broil the cauliflower steaks for an additional 2-3 minutes after roasting, but keep a close eye on them to prevent burning.
- For additional flavor, consider marinating the cauliflower steaks for 30 minutes before roasting.

Enjoy these delicious, roasted cauliflower steaks as a satisfying and flavorful dish!

Green Bean Almondine

Ingredients:

- 1 lb (450 g) fresh green beans, trimmed
- 3 tbsp unsalted butter or olive oil
- 1/4 cup sliced almonds
- 2 cloves garlic, minced
- 1 tbsp fresh lemon juice (about half a lemon)
- 1/2 tsp lemon zest (optional)
- Salt and black pepper to taste
- Fresh parsley or chives, chopped (optional, for garnish)

Instructions:

1. **Blanch the Green Beans:**
    - Bring a large pot of salted water to a boil.
    - Add the green beans and cook for 3-4 minutes, until they are bright green and tender-crisp.
    - Drain the green beans and immediately transfer them to a bowl of ice water to stop the cooking process. After a few minutes, drain again and pat dry with a paper towel.
2. **Toast the Almonds:**
    - In a large skillet, melt the butter or heat the olive oil over medium heat.
    - Add the sliced almonds and cook, stirring frequently, until they are golden brown and fragrant, about 2-3 minutes. Be careful not to burn them. Remove the almonds from the skillet and set aside.
3. **Sauté the Green Beans:**
    - In the same skillet, add a bit more butter or olive oil if needed.
    - Add the minced garlic and cook for about 30 seconds, until fragrant but not browned.
    - Add the blanched green beans to the skillet and cook for 3-4 minutes, tossing occasionally, until they are heated through and coated with the garlic.
4. **Combine and Finish:**
    - Stir in the toasted almonds.
    - Add the lemon juice and lemon zest, and toss to combine.
    - Season with salt and black pepper to taste.
5. **Serve:**
    - Transfer the green beans to a serving dish.
    - Garnish with chopped parsley or chives if desired.

Tips:

- **For Extra Flavor:** Add a pinch of red pepper flakes for a touch of heat or a splash of white wine vinegar for extra tang.
- **For a Nut-Free Version:** Simply omit the almonds or substitute with sunflower seeds for a similar crunch.

Enjoy this Green Bean Almondine as a sophisticated and tasty side dish that complements a variety of main courses!

Vegan Shepherd's Pie

Ingredients:

- **For the Vegetable Filling:**
    - 2 tbsp olive oil
    - 1 large onion, diced
    - 3 cloves garlic, minced
    - 2 carrots, diced
    - 2 celery stalks, diced
    - 1 cup mushrooms, diced
    - 1 cup frozen peas (or fresh peas)
    - 1 cup corn kernels (fresh, frozen, or canned)
    - 1 can (15 oz) lentils, drained and rinsed (or 1.5 cups cooked lentils)
    - 1 tbsp tomato paste
    - 2 tbsp soy sauce or tamari
    - 1 tbsp Worcestershire sauce (vegan, if needed)
    - 1 tsp dried thyme
    - 1/2 tsp dried rosemary
    - 1/2 tsp smoked paprika
    - Salt and black pepper to taste
    - 1 cup vegetable broth
    - 1 tbsp all-purpose flour or cornstarch (optional, for thickening)
- **For the Mashed Potatoes:**
    - 4 large potatoes, peeled and diced
    - 1/4 cup non-dairy milk (e.g., almond, soy, or oat milk)
    - 3 tbsp vegan butter or olive oil
    - Salt and black pepper to taste

Instructions:

1. **Prepare the Mashed Potatoes:**
    - Place the diced potatoes in a large pot and cover with water. Bring to a boil and cook until tender, about 15-20 minutes.
    - Drain the potatoes and return them to the pot.
    - Add non-dairy milk and vegan butter or olive oil. Mash until smooth and creamy. Season with salt and black pepper to taste. Set aside.
2. **Make the Vegetable Filling:**
    - Heat olive oil in a large skillet or saucepan over medium heat.
    - Add the diced onion and cook until softened, about 5 minutes.
    - Stir in the minced garlic, carrots, celery, and mushrooms. Cook for another 5-7 minutes, until the vegetables are tender.
    - Add the frozen peas, corn, and lentils. Stir well.

- Mix in the tomato paste, soy sauce, Worcestershire sauce, dried thyme, rosemary, smoked paprika, salt, and black pepper.
- Pour in the vegetable broth and bring to a simmer. Cook for 5 minutes, allowing the flavors to meld together.
- If you prefer a thicker filling, dissolve the flour or cornstarch in a little water and stir it into the mixture. Cook for another 2-3 minutes until thickened.

3. **Assemble and Bake:**
   - Preheat your oven to 400°F (200°C).
   - Transfer the vegetable filling to a baking dish.
   - Spread the mashed potatoes evenly over the top of the vegetable filling, smoothing out with a spatula.
   - Use a fork to create some texture on the surface of the mashed potatoes, which helps them get crispy.
4. **Bake:**
   - Bake in the preheated oven for 25-30 minutes, or until the top is golden brown and the filling is bubbling.
5. **Serve:**
   - Let the shepherd's pie cool for a few minutes before serving.

Tips:

- **For Extra Flavor:** Add a splash of white wine or a teaspoon of nutritional yeast to the vegetable filling for extra depth of flavor.
- **Vegetable Variations:** Feel free to swap in other vegetables you have on hand, such as parsnips, green beans, or butternut squash.

Enjoy this hearty and comforting Vegan Shepherd's Pie as a satisfying me

Mediterranean Quinoa Bowl

Ingredients:

- **For the Bowl:**
    - 1 cup quinoa
    - 2 cups water or vegetable broth
    - 1 cup cherry tomatoes, halved
    - 1 cucumber, diced
    - 1/2 red onion, diced
    - 1/2 cup Kalamata olives, pitted and sliced
    - 1/2 cup crumbled feta cheese (or vegan feta)
    - 1/4 cup fresh parsley, chopped
    - 1/4 cup fresh mint, chopped (optional)
- **For the Dressing:**
    - 1/4 cup extra-virgin olive oil
    - 2 tbsp lemon juice (about 1 lemon)
    - 1 clove garlic, minced
    - 1 tsp dried oregano
    - 1/2 tsp dried basil
    - Salt and black pepper to taste

Instructions:

1. **Cook the Quinoa:**
    - Rinse the quinoa under cold water.
    - In a medium saucepan, combine quinoa and water or vegetable broth. Bring to a boil.
    - Reduce heat to low, cover, and simmer for about 15 minutes, or until the quinoa is cooked and the liquid is absorbed.
    - Fluff with a fork and let it cool slightly.
2. **Prepare the Dressing:**
    - In a small bowl, whisk together olive oil, lemon juice, minced garlic, oregano, basil, salt, and black pepper.
3. **Assemble the Bowl:**
    - In a large bowl, combine the cooked quinoa, cherry tomatoes, cucumber, red onion, olives, and crumbled feta cheese.
    - Pour the dressing over the mixture and toss to combine.
    - Stir in the chopped parsley and mint if using.
4. **Serve:**
    - Serve immediately or refrigerate for later. The flavors meld together nicely after a few hours.

Tips:

- **For Extra Protein:** Add grilled chicken, chickpeas, or tofu.
- **For More Texture:** Toss in some toasted pine nuts or sunflower seeds.
- **Variations:** You can add roasted red peppers, artichoke hearts, or avocado for extra flavor and variety.

Enjoy this refreshing and satisfying Mediterranean Quinoa Bowl as a nutritious lunch or a light dinner!

Broccoli Cheddar Soup

Ingredients:

- **For the Soup:**
    - 2 tbsp butter or olive oil
    - 1 large onion, diced
    - 2 cloves garlic, minced
    - 4 cups broccoli florets (about 1 large head of broccoli)
    - 1 medium carrot, peeled and diced
    - 1 medium potato, peeled and diced
    - 4 cups vegetable broth or chicken broth
    - 1 cup shredded sharp cheddar cheese (or vegan cheese)
    - 1/2 cup heavy cream or non-dairy milk (for a lighter version, use almond or oat milk)
    - Salt and black pepper to taste
    - 1/4 tsp nutmeg (optional, for added warmth)
    - 1 tbsp all-purpose flour or cornstarch (optional, for thickening)
- **For Garnish (optional):**
    - Extra shredded cheddar cheese
    - Fresh parsley or chives

Instructions:

1. **Sauté the Aromatics:**
    - In a large pot, melt butter or heat olive oil over medium heat.
    - Add the diced onion and cook until softened, about 5 minutes.
    - Stir in the minced garlic and cook for another minute.
2. **Cook the Vegetables:**
    - Add the broccoli florets, diced carrot, and diced potato to the pot.
    - Pour in the vegetable or chicken broth and bring to a boil.
    - Reduce heat and simmer for 15-20 minutes, or until the vegetables are tender.
3. **Blend the Soup:**
    - Use an immersion blender to puree the soup directly in the pot until smooth. Alternatively, carefully transfer the soup in batches to a blender and blend until smooth. Return to the pot.
4. **Add Cheese and Cream:**
    - Stir in the shredded cheddar cheese and let it melt into the soup.
    - Add the heavy cream or non-dairy milk and mix well.
    - If you prefer a thicker soup, dissolve the flour or cornstarch in a little water and stir it into the soup. Cook for a few more minutes until thickened.
5. **Season and Serve:**
    - Season with salt, black pepper, and nutmeg (if using) to taste.

- Garnish with extra shredded cheddar cheese and fresh herbs if desired.

Tips:

- **For Extra Flavor:** Add a splash of hot sauce or a pinch of cayenne pepper for a bit of heat.
- **For Crunch:** Top with croutons or serve with a slice of crusty bread.

Enjoy this creamy Broccoli Cheddar Soup as a comforting meal perfect for chilly days!

Spinach and Feta Stuffed Mushrooms

Ingredients:

- **For the Stuffed Mushrooms:**
    - 12 large white or cremini mushrooms
    - 2 tbsp olive oil
    - 1 small onion, finely chopped
    - 2 cloves garlic, minced
    - 2 cups fresh spinach, chopped
    - 1/2 cup crumbled feta cheese (or vegan feta)
    - 1/4 cup breadcrumbs (optional, for added texture)
    - 1/4 cup grated Parmesan cheese (optional, or use vegan Parmesan)
    - Salt and black pepper to taste
    - 1/4 tsp dried oregano (optional)
    - Fresh parsley, chopped (for garnish)

Instructions:

1. **Prepare the Mushrooms:**
    - Preheat your oven to 375°F (190°C).
    - Clean the mushrooms with a damp paper towel. Remove the stems and set the caps aside. Finely chop the mushroom stems.
2. **Cook the Filling:**
    - Heat olive oil in a skillet over medium heat.
    - Add the chopped onion and cook until softened, about 5 minutes.
    - Stir in the minced garlic and cook for another minute.
    - Add the chopped mushroom stems and cook until they release their moisture and begin to brown, about 5-7 minutes.
    - Add the chopped spinach and cook until wilted, about 2-3 minutes. Remove from heat and let cool slightly.
3. **Mix the Filling:**
    - In a mixing bowl, combine the cooked mushroom mixture with crumbled feta cheese, breadcrumbs (if using), grated Parmesan (if using), salt, black pepper, and dried oregano (if using). Mix well.
4. **Stuff the Mushrooms:**
    - Place the mushroom caps on a baking sheet.
    - Spoon the spinach and feta mixture into each mushroom cap, pressing down gently to pack the filling.
5. **Bake:**
    - Bake the stuffed mushrooms in the preheated oven for 20-25 minutes, or until the mushrooms are tender and the tops are golden brown.
6. **Garnish and Serve:**

- Garnish with chopped fresh parsley before serving.

Tips:

- **For Extra Flavor:** You can add a pinch of red pepper flakes to the filling for a bit of heat.
- **For a Creamier Filling:** Stir in a tablespoon of cream cheese or Greek yogurt to the filling mixture.

Enjoy these Spinach and Feta Stuffed Mushrooms as a savory and satisfying treat!

Lentil and Vegetable Stew

Ingredients:

- **For the Stew:**
    - 2 tbsp olive oil
    - 1 large onion, diced
    - 3 cloves garlic, minced
    - 2 carrots, peeled and diced
    - 2 celery stalks, diced
    - 1 red bell pepper, diced
    - 1 cup mushrooms, sliced
    - 1 cup green or brown lentils, rinsed
    - 1 can (14.5 oz) diced tomatoes
    - 4 cups vegetable broth
    - 1 cup potatoes, peeled and diced (about 1 medium potato)
    - 1 cup frozen peas or corn (optional)
    - 1 tsp ground cumin
    - 1 tsp paprika
    - 1/2 tsp dried thyme
    - 1/2 tsp dried rosemary
    - 1 bay leaf
    - Salt and black pepper to taste
    - 1 tbsp balsamic vinegar or lemon juice (optional, for added flavor)
- **For Garnish (optional):**
    - Fresh parsley or cilantro, chopped
    - A dollop of plain yogurt or vegan yogurt

Instructions:

1. **Sauté the Aromatics:**
    - Heat olive oil in a large pot over medium heat.
    - Add the diced onion and cook until softened, about 5 minutes.
    - Stir in the minced garlic and cook for another minute.
2. **Cook the Vegetables:**
    - Add the carrots, celery, red bell pepper, and mushrooms to the pot. Cook for about 5-7 minutes, until the vegetables begin to soften.
3. **Add the Lentils and Seasonings:**
    - Stir in the rinsed lentils, diced tomatoes (with their juices), vegetable broth, potatoes, cumin, paprika, thyme, rosemary, bay leaf, salt, and black pepper.
    - Bring the mixture to a boil, then reduce heat and simmer, covered, for about 25-30 minutes, or until the lentils and potatoes are tender.
4. **Finish the Stew:**

- Stir in the frozen peas or corn, if using, and cook for an additional 5 minutes.
- Remove the bay leaf and stir in the balsamic vinegar or lemon juice, if desired, to brighten the flavors.

5. **Serve:**
    - Ladle the stew into bowls and garnish with fresh parsley or cilantro and a dollop of yogurt if desired.

Tips:

- **For Extra Depth:** Add a splash of soy sauce or a bit of smoked paprika for extra flavor.
- **For a Thicker Stew:** Mash some of the lentils and vegetables with a spoon or use an immersion blender to blend a portion of the stew.

This Lentil and Vegetable Stew is filling, flavorful, and packed with nutrients, making it a perfect choice for a wholesome and satisfying meal!

Tomato and Mozzarella Panini

Ingredients:

- **For the Panini:**
    - 1 loaf of ciabatta or sourdough bread (or 4 individual rolls)
    - 2 large ripe tomatoes, sliced
    - 8 oz fresh mozzarella cheese, sliced
    - Fresh basil leaves
    - 2 tbsp olive oil
    - 1 tbsp balsamic glaze or balsamic vinegar (optional)
    - Salt and black pepper to taste
    - 1 clove garlic, halved (optional, for rubbing on the bread)
- **For a Crispy Texture (optional):**
    - 1/4 cup grated Parmesan cheese

Instructions:

1. **Prepare the Ingredients:**
    - Preheat your panini press or a grill pan over medium heat.
    - Slice the ciabatta or sourdough bread into sandwich-sized pieces.
    - Slice the tomatoes and mozzarella cheese.
2. **Assemble the Panini:**
    - If using, rub the cut side of the garlic clove over one side of each slice of bread to infuse a subtle garlic flavor.
    - Drizzle olive oil on the inside of each slice of bread.
    - On the bottom half of each slice of bread, layer slices of fresh mozzarella cheese, tomato slices, and fresh basil leaves.
    - Drizzle with balsamic glaze or balsamic vinegar if using. Season with salt and black pepper.
3. **Grill the Panini:**
    - Place the top half of the bread on the sandwich.
    - If you're using a panini press, place the sandwiches in the press and cook according to the manufacturer's instructions, usually 3-5 minutes, until the bread is crispy and the cheese is melted.
    - If using a grill pan, place the sandwiches in the pan and press down with a heavy object or another pan. Cook for 3-4 minutes on each side, or until the bread is golden and the cheese is melted.
4. **Optional: Add Parmesan:**
    - For an extra crispy texture, sprinkle the outside of the bread with grated Parmesan cheese before grilling.
5. **Serve:**
    - Cut the panini in half and serve warm.

Tips:

- **For Added Flavor:** Try adding a layer of pesto or a slice of cooked bacon.
- **For a Healthier Option:** Use whole-grain bread and part-skim mozzarella cheese.

Enjoy your Tomato and Mozzarella Panini as a tasty and satisfying sandwich that's perfect for lunch or a light dinner!

Apple and Walnut Salad

Ingredients:

- **For the Salad:**
    - 4 cups mixed salad greens (e.g., arugula, spinach, or baby greens)
    - 2 large apples (e.g., Honeycrisp, Fuji, or Gala), cored and thinly sliced
    - 1/2 cup walnuts, toasted
    - 1/4 cup crumbled feta cheese (or goat cheese) (optional)
    - 1/4 cup dried cranberries or raisins
    - 1/4 red onion, thinly sliced
    - 1/4 cup thinly sliced celery (optional)
    - 1/4 cup chopped fresh parsley or mint (optional)
- **For the Dressing:**
    - 3 tbsp extra-virgin olive oil
    - 2 tbsp apple cider vinegar or white wine vinegar
    - 1 tbsp honey or maple syrup (for a vegan option)
    - 1 tsp Dijon mustard
    - Salt and black pepper to taste

Instructions:

1. **Prepare the Salad Ingredients:**
    - In a large salad bowl, combine the mixed greens, sliced apples, toasted walnuts, crumbled feta cheese (if using), dried cranberries, red onion, and celery (if using).
2. **Make the Dressing:**
    - In a small bowl or jar, whisk together the olive oil, apple cider vinegar, honey or maple syrup, Dijon mustard, salt, and black pepper until well combined.
3. **Toss and Serve:**
    - Drizzle the dressing over the salad and toss gently to combine, ensuring all ingredients are well coated.
    - Garnish with fresh parsley or mint if desired.
4. **Serve:**
    - Serve immediately for the freshest taste. If preparing in advance, keep the dressing separate and add it just before serving to prevent the salad from becoming soggy.

Tips:

- **For Extra Crunch:** Add some thinly sliced radishes or a handful of sunflower seeds.
- **For a Protein Boost:** Add grilled chicken or chickpeas to make it a more substantial meal.

- **For Variation:** Try different types of apples or add other fruits like pears or pomegranate seeds for a unique twist.

This Apple and Walnut Salad is a delightful combination of sweet, tangy, and crunchy elements, making it a flavorful and satisfying addition to any meal!

www.ingramcontent.com/pod-product-compliance
Lightning Source LLC
LaVergne TN
LVHW081611060526
838201LV00054B/2204